WHAT'S COOKING?

INDIAN

First published in Great Britain in 1997 by
Parragon
Unit 13–17
Avonbridge Trading Estate
Atlantic Road
Avonmouth
Bristol BS11 9QD

ISBN: 0-7525-2253-1

Produced by Haldane Mason, London

Acknowledgements
Art Director: Ron Samuels
Designer: Errol Campbell
Editors: Jo-Anne Cox, Charles Dixon-Spain
Photography: Karl Adamson, Iain Bagwell, Martin
Brigdale, Joff Lee

Printed in Italy

Material in this book has previously appeared in
Classic Indian Cooking and *Indian Side Dishes* by
Cara Hobday and *Indian Vegetarian Cooking* by
Louise Steele

Note
Cup measurements in this book are for
American cups. Tablespoons are assumed to be
15 ml. Unless otherwise stated, milk is assumed
to be full-fat, eggs are standard size 3 and
pepper is freshly ground black pepper.

CONTENTS

Introduction

Indian cuisine is enjoyed all over the world, not least for the many subtle combinations of aromatic flavourings and spices that are used in its dishes. From the delicious but very hot Vindaloo Curry to the subtly aromatic Kashmiri Spinach, this book takes you on a journey through one of the most exciting cuisines in the world.

For many there is an art to Indian cooking; dealing with over thirty different spices and flavourings can be intimidating, but the tastes and smells drifting up from your pans will encourage you to continue. The spices themselves are called *masalas*. Once ground together, masalas can keep for up to two months, but it is best to mix and use them fresh. Garam Masala is often used in the recipes here and involves grinding the following spices together: 1 tsp cardamom seeds, 2 tsp cloves, 2 tbsp cumin seeds, 2 tbsp coriander seeds, 2 dried bay leaves, 7.5 cm/ 3 inch cinnamon stick, 1 tbsp black peppercorns and 1 dried red chilli. It is advisable to prepare your dishes in advance as the spices and flavourings will take time to realize their full potential. Make the dish and leave it overnight or for up to three days in the refrigerator before being re-heated. A common accompaniment to spicy Indian dishes is Cucumber Raita. This is simple to make – simply mix together 250 g/8 oz/1 cup natural yogurt, 2 tsp chopped fresh mint, 175 g/6 oz cucumber, peeled, deseeded and cut into matchsticks, and salt to taste.

Variety and contrast in your meals as a whole is paramount. To this end this book takes recipes from all over the Indian sub-continent to provide a surprising and delicious mixture of tastes and aromas. First are the samosas, pakoras and delicate starters, then the meats. Fish and seafood add a lighter texture to the recipes that follow, before the rice and vegetables which can act as side-dishes or the main event, depending upon your tastes. Palate-cleansing desserts finish the book, and offer the cook several delicious final flourishes.

Garlicky Mushroom Pakoras

Whole button mushrooms are dunked in a spiced garlicky batter and deep fried until golden.

SERVES 6

175 g/ 6 oz/ 1½ cups gram flour • ½ tsp salt
¼ tsp baking powder • 1 tsp cumin seeds
½–1 tsp chilli powder, to taste
200 ml/ 7 fl oz/ ¾ cup water
2 garlic cloves, crushed • 1 small onion, finely chopped
vegetable oil, for deep frying
500 g/ 1 lb button mushrooms, trimmed and wiped

To garnish:
lemon wedges • sprigs of coriander (cilantro)

1 Put the gram flour, salt, baking powder, cumin and chilli powder into a bowl and mix together. Make a well in the centre and gradually stir in the water, to form a batter.

2 Stir the crushed garlic and the chopped onion into the batter and leave the mixture to infuse for 10 minutes. One-third fill a deep-fat fryer with vegetable oil and heat to 180°C/350°F or until a cube of day-old bread is browned in 30 seconds. Lower the basket into the oil.

3 Meanwhile, mix the mushrooms into the batter, stirring to coat. Remove a few at a time and place them into the hot oil. Fry for about 2 minutes or until golden brown.

4 Remove from the pan with a slotted spoon and drain on paper towels while cooking the remainder in the same way. Serve hot, sprinkled with coarse salt and garnished with lemon wedges and sprigs of coriander (cilantro).

Samosas

Each filling recipe makes enough to fill all the pastry.

MAKES 32

Pastry:
500 g/ 1 lb/ 4 cups plain (all-purpose) flour
½ tsp turmeric • ½ tsp salt
100 g/ 3½ oz/ scant ½ cup ghee
*about 200 ml/ 7 fl oz/ ¾ cup milk, mixed with a little
lemon juice*

Tuna filling:
½ tsp each of turmeric and cayenne • 1 tsp ground cumin
1 tsp ground coriander • 200 g/ 7 oz can of tuna, drained
60 g/ 2 oz/ ⅓ cup frozen peas, cooked
60 g/ 2 oz/ ½ cup boiled potatoes, diced • salt and pepper

Vegetarian filling:
250 g/ 8 oz white potatoes, boiled
½ × 425 g/ 14 oz can of artichoke hearts, drained and puréed
1 tsp ground black pepper • 2 tsp coriander seeds, ground
1 tsp cumin seeds, ground • ½ tsp fenugreek seeds, ground
2 large tomatoes, peeled and deseeded
90 g/ 3 oz/ ½ cup frozen peas, cooked • salt and pepper

Sauce:
6 anchovies • 2 tbsp natural yogurt • salt and pepper

1 To make the tuna filling, roast the spices in a large frying pan (skillet). Remove from the heat and add the tuna, peas and potatoes. Stir well and season. Continue from step 3.

2 To make the vegetarian filling, mash the potatoes and combine with the artichokes. Roast the spices in a large frying pan (skillet). Remove from the heat and add the potato mixture. Stir

well to combine. Chop the tomatoes and carefully fold in with the peas. Season.

3 Roll out the pastry and cut out 16 × 12 cm/ 5 inch circles. Cut each circle in half and put a teaspoonful of filling on each half. Brush the edges with the milk and lemon and fold each half over to form a triangle. Seal well, and crimp the edges. Bake in a preheated oven at 190°C/ 375°F/Gas mark 5.

4 To make the sauce, mash the anchovies, mix with the yogurt and season. Serve with the hot samosas.

Spicy Bites

Here are three delicious morsels to whet your appetite before a meal. Use courgettes (zucchini) with the flowers still attached.

SERVES 4

Spiced nuts:

*125 g/ 4 oz/ 1 cup mixed nuts, such as peanuts,
cashews and blanched almonds • 1 dried red chilli
1 tsp sunflower oil • 1 garlic clove • ½ tsp salt
1 tsp Garam Masala (see page 4) • ½ tsp clear honey*

Deep-fried courgettes (zucchini):

*125 g/ 4 oz/ 1 cup plain (all-purpose) flour
½ tsp each turmeric and cayenne pepper
150 ml/ ¼ pint/ ⅔ cup water • 2 eggs
vegetable oil • 1 courgette (zucchini), cut into batons*

Mussel morsels:

*1 kg/ 2 lb small mussels, scrubbed
3 tbsp mayonnaise • 1 tsp Garam Masala (see page 4)
½ red chilli, deseeded and chopped finely
2 spring onions (scallions), chopped finely
45 g/ 1½ oz/ ¾ cup white breadcrumbs • salt*

Spiced Nuts

1 Cook the nuts in a dry, heavy-based pan over a moderate heat until the oil is released, about 5 minutes. Add the remaining ingredients except the honey, and cook for 3 minutes, stirring. Add the honey and cook for 2 minutes. Remove from heat and turn into a serving dish.

Deep-Fried Courgettes (Zucchini)

1 Sift the flour and spices together. Add the water, eggs and 1 tablespoon of oil. Whisk until smooth. Heat a little oil in a wok. Dip the batons into the batter, and carefully drop into the oil. When cooked, remove and drain on paper towels.

Mussel Morsels

1 Put a little water into a large pan. Discard any mussels that are not closed. Add the mussels and cover the pan. Cook over a high heat for 5 minutes; do not uncover. Drain the mussels and discard any unopened ones. Remove the shells and reserve them. Chop the mussel meat finely. Stir the mayonnaise into the mussel meat. Add the remaining ingredients and season to taste. Spoon the mixture back into the shells, and arrange on a serving plate.

Butterfly Prawns (Shrimp)

These prawns (shrimp) look stunning when presented on the skewers, and make an impressive prelude to a meal.

SERVES 4

8 wooden skewers
500 g/ 1 lb or 16 raw tiger prawns (shrimp), shelled, leaving tails intact
juice of 2 limes • 1 tsp cardamom seeds
2 tsp cumin seeds, ground
2 tsp coriander seeds, ground
½ tsp ground cinnamon • 1 tsp ground turmeric
1 tsp cayenne pepper • 1 garlic clove, crushed
2 tbsp oil • cucumber slices, to garnish

1 Soak 8 wooden skewers in water for 20 minutes to prevent them from scorching. Cut the prawns (shrimp) lengthways in half down to the tail, so that they flatten out to a symmetrical shape.

2 Thread a prawn (shrimp) on to 2 wooden skewers, with the tail between them, so that the skewers hold the prawn (shrimp) in shape. Thread another 3 prawns (shrimp) on to these 2 skewers in the same way. Repeat with the remaining prawns (shrimp) and skewers until you have 4 sets of 4 prawns (shrimps) each.

3 Lay the skewered prawns (shrimp) in a non-porous, non-metallic dish, and sprinkle over the lime juice.

4 Mix the spices, garlic and oil, and coat the prawns (shrimp) in the mixture. Cover and chill for 4 hours.

5 Cook over a hot barbecue or in a grill (broiler) pan lined with foil under a preheated grill (broiler) for 6 minutes, turning once.

6 Serve immediately, garnished with cucumber slices and accompanied by a sweet chutney.

Chicken Jalfrezi

This is a quick and tasty way to use leftover roast chicken. The sauce can also be used for any cooked poultry, lamb or beef.

SERVES 4

1 tsp mustard oil • 3 tbsp vegetable oil
1 large onion, chopped finely • 3 garlic cloves, crushed
1 tbsp tomato purée (paste)
2 tomatoes, skinned and chopped
1 tsp ground turmeric
½ tsp cumin seeds, ground
½ tsp coriander seeds, ground
½ tsp chilli powder • ½ tsp Garam Masala (see page 4)
1 tsp red wine vinegar
1 small red (bell) pepper, chopped
125 g/ 4 oz/ 1 cup frozen broad (fava) beans
500 g/ 1 lb cooked chicken, cut into bite-sized pieces
salt • sprigs of fresh coriander (cilantro), to garnish
cooked rice, to serve

1 Heat the mustard oil in a large frying pan (skillet) set over a high heat for 1 minute until it begins to smoke. Add the vegetable oil, reduce the heat and then add the onion and garlic. Fry the garlic and onion until golden.

2 Add the tomato purée (paste), chopped tomatoes, turmeric, ground cumin and coriander seeds, chilli powder, garam masala and vinegar to the frying pan (skillet). Stir the mixture until fragrant.

3 Add the red (bell) pepper and broad (fava) beans and stir for 2 minutes until the pepper is softened. Stir in the chicken, and salt to taste. Simmer gently for 6–8 minutes until the chicken is heated through and the beans are tender. Garnish with coriander (cilantro) sprigs and serve with cooked rice.

Tandoori Chicken

To replicate the traditional tandoor oven, cook this chicken at a very high temperature, preferably on a barbecue.

SERVES 4

8 small chicken pieces, skinned • 3 dried red chillies
1 tsp salt • 2 tsp coriander seeds
2 tbsp lime juice • 2 garlic cloves, crushed
2.5 cm/1 inch piece of ginger root, grated • 1 clove
2 tsp Garam Masala (see page 4) • 2 tsp chilli powder
½ onion, chopped
300 ml/½ pint/1¼ cups natural yogurt
1 tbsp chopped fresh coriander (cilantro)
lemon slices, to garnish
Cucumber Raita (see page 4), to serve

1 Make 2–3 slashes with a sharp knife in the flesh of the chicken pieces.

2 Crush together the chillies, salt, coriander seeds, lime juice, garlic, ginger and clove. Stir in the garam masala and chilli powder. Transfer to a small saucepan and heat gently until aromatic. Add the onion and fry. Stir in the yogurt and remove the pan from the heat.

3 Arrange the chicken in a non-metallic dish and pour over the yogurt mixture. Cover and leave in the refrigerator to marinate for 4 hours or overnight.

4 Arrange the chicken on a grill (broiler) tray and cook under a preheated very hot grill (broiler) or over a barbecue for 20–30 minutes, turning once, until the chicken juices run clear when the thickest parts of the portions are pierced with a sharp knife.

5 Sprinkle the chicken with chopped fresh coriander (cilantro). Serve hot or cold, garnished with the lemon slices and accompanied by cucumber raita.

Chicken Tikka Masala

**Serve this rich dish with accompaniments
to provide a balance to the fiery flavours.**

SERVES 4

*8 skewers • ½ onion, chopped coarsely
60 g/ 2 oz/ 4 tbsp tomato purée (paste) • 1 tsp cumin seeds
2.5 cm/ 1 inch piece of ginger root, chopped
3 tbsp lemon juice • 2 garlic cloves, crushed
2 tsp chilli powder • 750 g/ 1½ lb boneless chicken
salt and pepper • sprigs of fresh mint, to garnish*

Masala sauce:
*2 tbsp ghee • 1 onion, sliced
1 tbsp black onion seeds • 3 garlic cloves, crushed
2 fresh green chillies, chopped
200 g/ 7 oz can tomatoes
120 ml/ 4 fl oz/ ½ cup natural yogurt
120 ml/ 4 fl oz/ ½ cup coconut milk
1 tbsp chopped fresh coriander (cilantro)
1 tbsp chopped fresh mint • 2 tbsp lemon or lime juice
½ tsp Garam Masala (see page 4) • vegetable oil*

1 Purée the onion, tomato purée (paste), cumin, ginger, lemon juice, garlic, chilli powder, salt and pepper in a blender and transfer to a bowl. Alternatively, grind the cumin with a pestle and mortar and transfer to a bowl. Chop the onion and ginger and stir into the bowl with the tomato purée (paste), lemon juice, salt and pepper, garlic and chilli powder.

2 Cut chicken into 5 cm/ 2 inch cubes. Stir into the spiced mixture and leave to marinate for 2 hours.

3 Make the masala sauce. Heat the ghee in a large saucepan, add the onion and stir over a medium heat for 5 minutes. Add the onion seeds, garlic and chillies and cook until aromatic. Add the tomatoes, yogurt and

coconut milk, and simmer for 20 minutes.

4 Meanwhile, divide the marinated chicken evenly between 8 oiled skewers and cook under a preheated very hot grill (broiler) for 15 minutes, turning frequently. Remove the chicken from the skewers and add to the masala sauce. Stir in the coriander (cilantro), mint, lemon or lime juice, and garam masala. Serve garnished with sprigs of mint.

Lamb Biryani

In India this elaborate, beautifully coloured dish is usually served on festive occasions.

SERVES 4

250 g/ 8 oz/ 1¼ cups basmati rice, rinsed and soaked in cold water for 30 minutes
2 garlic cloves, peeled and left whole
2.5 cm/ 1 inch piece of ginger root, grated • 4 cloves
2 green cardamom pods • ½ tsp black peppercorns
1 tsp cumin seeds • 1 tsp coriander seeds
2.5 cm/ 1 inch piece cinnamon stick
1 tsp saffron strands • 50 ml/ 2 fl oz/ 4 tbsp tepid water
2 tbsp ghee • 2 shallots, sliced
¼ tsp grated nutmeg • ¼ tsp chilli powder
500 g/ 1 lb boneless lamb, cut into 2.5 cm/ 1 inch cubes
180 ml/ 6 fl oz/ ¾ cup natural yogurt
30 g/ 1 oz/ 2 tbsp sultanas (golden raisins)
30 g/ 1 oz/ ¼ cup flaked (slivered) almonds, toasted

1 Bring a large saucepan of salted water to the boil. Add the rice and boil for 6 minutes. Drain and set aside.

2 Grind together the garlic, ginger, cloves, cardamom pods, peppercorns, cumin, coriander and cinnamon.

3 Combine the saffron and water, and set aside. Heat the ghee in a large saucepan and add the shallots. Fry until golden brown then add the ground spice mix, nutmeg and chilli powder. Stir for 1 minute and add the lamb. Cook until evenly browned. Add the yogurt, stirring constantly, then the sultanas (golden raisins) and bring to a simmer. Cook for 40 minutes, stirring occasionally.

4 Carefully pile the rice on top of the sauce in the pan, in a pyramid shape. Trickle the saffron solution over the rice in lines. Cover the pan with a clean tea towel and put on the lid. Reduce

the heat to low and cook for 10 minutes. Remove the lid and tea towel, and quickly make 3 holes in the rice with a wooden spoon handle, to the level of the sauce, but not touching it. Replace the tea towel and the lid and leave to stand for 5 minutes.

5 Remove the lid and tea towel, lightly fork the rice and serve, sprinkled with the toasted almonds.

Lamb Do Pyaza

Do Pyaza usually indicates a dish of meat cooked with onions, and in this recipe the onions are cooked in two different ways.

SERVES 4

2 tbsp ghee • 2 large onions, sliced finely
4 garlic cloves, 2 of them crushed
750 g/ 1½ lb boneless lamb, cut into 2.5 cm/ 1 inch cubes
1 tsp chilli powder
2.5 cm/ 1 inch piece of ginger root, grated
2 fresh green chillies, chopped • ½ tsp ground turmeric
180 ml/ 6 fl oz/ ¾ cup natural yogurt • 2 cloves
2.5 cm/ 1 inch piece cinnamon stick
300 ml/ ½ pint/ 1¼ cups water
2 tbsp chopped fresh coriander (cilantro)
3 tbsp lemon juice • salt and pepper
naan bread, to serve

1 Heat the ghee in a large pan and add 1 of the onions and all the garlic. Cook for 2–3 minutes, stirring constantly. Add the lamb and brown all over. Remove the lamb and set aside.

2 Add the chilli powder, ginger, chillies and turmeric and stir for a further 30 seconds. Season to taste, then add the yogurt, cloves, cinnamon and water. Return the lamb to the pan. Bring to the boil then simmer for 10 minutes.

3 Transfer the mixture to an ovenproof dish and cook uncovered in a preheated oven, 180°C/ 350°F/Gas Mark 4, for 40 minutes. Adjust the seasoning, if necessary.

4 Stir in the remaining onion and cook for a further 40 minutes. Add the fresh coriander (cilantro) and lemon juice, and stir. Serve hot, accompanied by naan bread.

Vindaloo Curry

Vindaloo is the classic fiery curry from Goa.

SERVES 4

100 ml/ 3½ fl oz/ scant ½ cup oil
1 large onion, sliced into half rings
120 ml/ 4 fl oz/ ½ cup white wine vinegar
300 ml/ ½ pint/ 1¼ cups water
750 g/ 1½ lb boneless pork, diced • 2 tsp cumin seeds
4 dried red chillies • 1 tsp black peppercorns
6 green cardamom pods
2.5 cm/ 1 inch piece cinnamon stick
1 tsp black mustard seeds • 3 cloves
1 tsp fenugreek seeds • 2 tbsp ghee
4 garlic cloves, chopped finely
3.5 cm/ 1½ inch piece of ginger root, chopped finely
1 tbsp coriander seeds, ground
2 tomatoes, skinned and chopped
250 g/ 8 oz potato, cut into 1 cm/ ½ inch cubes
1 tsp light brown sugar • ½ tsp ground turmeric
salt • basmati rice and pickles, to serve

1 Heat the oil in a large saucepan and fry the onion until golden brown. Set aside.

2 Combine 2 tablespoons of the vinegar with 1 tablespoon of the water in a large bowl. Add the pork and mix well. Set aside.

3 In a blender mix the onion, cumin, chillies, peppercorns, cardamom, cinnamon, mustard seeds, cloves and fenugreek to a paste. Alternatively, grind the ingredients together with a pestle and mortar. Transfer to a bowl and add the remaining vinegar.

4 Heat the ghee in a frying pan (skillet) or casserole, add the pork and cook until it is browned on all sides. Add the garlic, ginger and ground coriander and stir

until fragrant. Add the tomatoes, potato, brown sugar, turmeric and remaining water. Add salt to taste and bring to the boil. Stir in the spice paste, cover and reduce the heat, and simmer for 1 hour. Serve with basmati rice and pickles.

Green Fish Curry

This dish is from southern India. It has a wonderful fresh, hot, exotic taste resulting from the generous amount of fresh herbs, sharp fresh chillies and coconut milk.

SERVES 4

1 tbsp oil
2 spring onions (scallions), sliced
1 tsp cumin seeds, ground
2 fresh green chillies, chopped
1 tsp coriander seeds, ground
4 tbsp chopped fresh coriander (cilantro)
4 tbsp chopped fresh mint
1 tbsp chopped chives
150 ml/¼ pint/⅔ cup coconut milk
4 white fish fillets, about 250 g/8 oz each
salt and pepper
basmati rice, to serve
1 sprig of mint, to garnish

1 Heat the oil in a large frying pan (skillet) or shallow saucepan and add the spring onions (scallions). Stir-fry over a medium heat until they are softened but not coloured.

2 Stir in the cumin, chillies and ground coriander, and cook until aromatic. Add the fresh coriander (cilantro), mint, chives and coconut milk and season with salt and pepper to taste.

3 Carefully place the fish in the pan and poach for 10–15 minutes until the flesh flakes when tested with a fork.

4 Serve the fish curry with basmati rice and garnish with a mint sprig.

Prawn (Shrimp) Bhuna

**This is a fiery recipe with subtle
undertones. As the flavour of the prawns
(shrimp) should be noticeable, the spices
should not take over this dish.**

SERVES 4–6

2 dried red chillies, deseeded if liked
3 fresh green chillies, finely chopped
1 tsp ground turmeric
2 tsp white wine vinegar
½ tsp salt
3 garlic cloves, crushed
½ tsp pepper • 1 tsp paprika
500 g/ 1 lb uncooked peeled king prawns (shrimp)
4 tbsp oil
1 onion, chopped very finely
180 ml/ 6 fl oz/ ¾ cup water
2 tbsp lemon juice
2 tsp Garam Masala (see page 4)
sprigs of fresh coriander (cilantro), to garnish

1 Combine the chillies,
turmeric, vinegar, salt,
garlic, pepper and paprika in
a non-metallic bowl. Stir in
the prawns (shrimp) and leave
to marinate for 10 minutes.

2 Heat the oil in a large
frying pan (skillet) or wok,
add the onion and fry for
3–4 minutes until soft.

3 Add the prawns (shrimp)
and spice mixture to the
pan and stir-fry over a high
heat for 2 minutes.

4 Reduce the heat, add the
water and boil for 10
minutes, stirring occasionally,
until the water has
evaporated and the curry is
fragrant. Stir in the lemon
juice and garam masala.

5 Garnish with sprigs of
fresh coriander (cilantro)
and serve with rice.

Curried Crab

Shellfish is a major part of the diet in coastal areas of India. It is frozen and shipped to all parts India, to be used in a wide variety of dishes.

SERVES 4

2 tbsp mustard oil • 1 tbsp ghee
1 onion, chopped finely
5 cm/2 inch piece of ginger root, grated
2 garlic cloves, peeled but left whole
1 tsp ground turmeric • 1 tsp salt
1 tsp chilli powder
2 fresh green chillies, chopped
1 tsp paprika
125 g/4 oz/½ cup brown crab meat
350 g/12 oz/1½ cups white crab meat
250 ml/8 fl oz/1 cup natural yogurt
1 tsp Garam Masala (see page 4) • basmati rice, to serve
fresh coriander (cilantro), to garnish

1 Heat the mustard oil in a large, preferably non-stick, frying pan (skillet), wok or saucepan. When it starts to smoke add the ghee and onion. Stir for 3 minutes over a medium heat until the onion has softened.

2 Stir in the ginger and whole garlic cloves. Add the turmeric, salt, chilli powder, chillies and paprika. Mix thoroughly.

3 Increase the heat and add the crab meat and yogurt. Simmer, stirring occasionally, for 10 minutes until the sauce has thickened slightly. Add garam masala to taste.

4 Serve hot, over plain basmati rice, and garnished with fresh coriander (cilantro).

Masala Fried Fish

Frying fish is classically Indian, although it does not always spring to mind when thinking of Indian food.

SERVES 4–8

8 plaice or other white fish fillets, about
125–150 g/4–5 oz each
1 tbsp ground turmeric • 2 tbsp plain (all-purpose) flour
salt • ½ tsp black peppercorns, ground
1 tsp chilli powder • 1 tbsp coriander seeds, ground
1 garlic clove, crushed • 2 tsp Garam Masala (see page 4)
oil for deep frying

To garnish:
chilli powder • lemon wedges

1 To skin the fish fillets, lay the fillet skin side down with the tail nearest you. Hold the tail end between your thumb and forefinger. Hold a sharp knife at a shallow angle to the fish in your other hand. Make an angled cut between the flesh and skin, then continue to cut the flesh from the skin until it is free.

2 In a shallow dish, combine the turmeric, flour, salt to taste, peppercorns, chilli powder, coriander seeds, garlic and garam masala. Mix well.

3 Fill a saucepan or a frying pan (skillet) with oil to a depth of 5–7 cm/2–3 inches, and heat to 180°C/350°F.

4 Coat the fish fillets in the spice mix either by shaking gently in a paper bag or turning over in the dish until well coated. Deep fry the fish fillets for about 3–5 minutes, turning often until the fish flakes easily with a fork. Drain on paper towels.

5 Serve sprinkled with chilli powder, garnished with lemon wedges.

Muttar Paneer

**Paneer is a delicious fresh, soft cheese
frequently used in Indian cooking.**

SERVES 4

150 ml/¼ pint/⅔ cup vegetable oil
2 onions, chopped • 2 garlic cloves, crushed
2.5 cm/1 inch piece of ginger root, chopped finely
1 tsp Garam Masala (see page 4) • 1 tsp ground turmeric
1 tsp chilli powder • 500 g/1 lb frozen peas
200 g/7 oz can of chopped tomatoes
120 ml/4 fl oz/½ cup vegetable stock
salt and pepper • 2 tbsp chopped fresh coriander
(cilantro), to garnish

Paneer:
2.5 litres/4 pints/10 cups milk • 5 tbsp lemon juice
1 garlic clove, crushed (optional)
1 tbsp chopped fresh coriander (cilantro) (optional)

1 To make the paneer, bring the milk to a rolling boil in a large saucepan. Remove from the heat and stir in the lemon juice. Return to the heat for about 1 minute until the curds and whey separate. Remove from the heat. Line a colander with double thickness muslin and pour the mixture through the muslin. Add the garlic and coriander, if using. Squeeze all the liquid from the curds and leave to drain. Transfer to a dish, cover with a plate and weights and leave overnight in the refrigerator.

2 Cut the pressed paneer into small cubes. Heat the oil in a large frying pan, add the paneer cubes and fry until golden on all sides. Remove from the pan and drain on paper towels.

3 Pour off some of the oil, leaving 4 tablespoons in the pan. Add the onions, garlic and ginger and fry for 5 minutes, stirring frequently.

Stir in the garam masala, turmeric and chilli powder and fry for 2 minutes. Add the peas, tomatoes and stock, and season. Cover and simmer for 10 minutes, stirring, until the onion is tender.

4 Add the fried paneer cubes and cook for a further 5 minutes. Taste and adjust the seasoning, if necessary. Sprinkle with the coriander (cilantro) and serve at once.

Spiced Basmati Pilau

Omit the broccoli and mushrooms if you want a simple spiced pilau. Remove the whole spices before serving.

SERVES 6

500 g/ 1 lb/ 2½ cups basmati rice
175 g/ 6 oz broccoli • 6 tbsp vegetable oil
2 large onions, chopped
250 g/ 8 oz mushrooms, wiped and sliced
2 garlic cloves, crushed • 6 cardamom pods, split
6 whole cloves • 8 black peppercorns
1 cinnamon stick or piece of cassia bark
1 tsp ground turmeric
1.25 litres/ 2¼ pints/ 5 cups boiling vegetable stock or water
60 g/ 2 oz/ ⅓ cup seedless raisins
60 g/ 2 oz/ ½ cup unsalted pistachios, coarsely chopped
salt and pepper

1 Place the rice in a sieve and rinse under cold running water until the water runs clear. Drain. Trim off the broccoli stalk and cut into florets, then quarter the stalk lengthways and cut diagonally into 1 cm/½ inch pieces.

2 Heat the oil in a large saucepan, add the onions and broccoli stalks and cook for 3 minutes, stirring often. Add the mushrooms, rice, garlic and spices and cook for 1 minute, stirring often until the rice is coated in oil.

3 Add the boiling stock and season with salt and pepper. Stir in the broccoli florets and bring the mixture back to the boil. Cover, reduce the heat and cook gently for 15 minutes.

4 Remove from the heat and leave to stand for 5 minutes, covered. Add the raisins and pistachios and gently fork through to fluff up the grains. Serve hot.

Curried Okra

Okra, also known as bhindi and ladies' fingers, are a favourite Indian vegetable. They are now widely available.

SERVES 4

500 g/ 1 lb fresh okra
4 tbsp vegetable ghee or oil
1 bunch spring onions (scallions), trimmed and sliced
2 garlic cloves, crushed
5 cm/ 2 inch piece of ginger root, chopped finely
1 tsp minced chilli (from a jar)
1½ tsp ground cumin
1 tsp ground coriander
1 tsp ground turmeric
200 g/ 7 oz can of chopped tomatoes
150 ml/ ¼ pint/ ⅔ cup vegetable stock
1 tsp Garam Masala (see page 4)
salt and pepper
chopped fresh coriander (cilantro), to garnish

1 Rinse the okra, trim off the stalks and pat dry.

2 Heat the ghee or oil in a large pan, add the spring onions (scallions), garlic, ginger and chilli and fry gently for 1 minute, stirring frequently.

3 Stir in the ground cumin, coriander and turmeric and fry gently for 30 seconds, then add the tomatoes, stock and okra. Season with salt and pepper to taste and simmer for about 15 minutes, stirring and turning the mixture occasionally. The okra should be cooked but still a little crisp.

4 Sprinkle with the garam masala, taste and adjust the seasoning, if necessary.

5 Garnish with the chopped coriander (cilantro) and serve hot.

Aubergine (Eggplant) in Saffron Sauce

Here is a quick and simple, delicately spiced and delicious way to cook aubergine (eggplant).

SERVES 4

a good pinch of saffron strands, crushed
1 tbsp boiling water
1 large aubergine (eggplant)
3 tbsp vegetable oil
1 large onion, coarsely chopped
2 garlic cloves, crushed
2.5 cm/1 inch piece of ginger root, chopped
1½ tbsp mild or medium curry paste
1 tsp cumin seeds
150 ml/¼ pint/⅔ cup double (heavy) cream
150 ml/¼ pint/⅔ cup strained thick yogurt
2 tbsp mango chutney, chopped if necessary
salt and pepper

1 Place the saffron in a small bowl, add the boiling water and leave to infuse for at least 5 minutes.

2 Trim the leaf end off the aubergine (eggplant), cut lengthways into quarters, then into 1 cm/½ inch thick slices.

3 Heat the oil in a large frying pan (skillet), add the onion and cook gently for 3 minutes. Stir in the aubergine (eggplant), garlic, ginger, curry paste and cumin, and cook gently for 3 minutes.

4 Stir in the saffron solution, cream, yogurt and chutney, and cook gently for 8–10 minutes, stirring frequently, until the aubergine (eggplant) is cooked through and tender. Season with salt and pepper to taste and serve hot.

Fried Spiced Potatoes

A deliciously good accompaniment to almost any main course dish.

SERVES 4

2 onions, chopped coarsely
5 cm/2 inch piece of ginger root, chopped • 2 garlic cloves
2–3 tbsp mild or medium curry paste
4 tbsp water • 750 g/1½ lb new potatoes
vegetable oil, for deep frying
3 tbsp vegetable ghee or oil
150 ml/¼ pint/⅔ cup strained thick yogurt
150 ml/¼ pint/⅔ cup double (heavy) cream
3 tbsp chopped fresh mint • salt and pepper
spring onions (scallions), trimmed and sliced, to garnish

1 Place the onions, ginger, garlic, curry paste and water in a blender or food processor and process until smooth.

2 Cut the potatoes into quarters – the pieces need to be about 2.5 cm/1 inch in size – and pat dry with paper towels.

3 Heat the oil in a deep-fat fryer to 180°C/350°F and fry the potatoes, in batches, for about 5 minutes or until golden brown, turning frequently. Remove from the pan and drain on paper towels.

4 Heat the ghee or oil in a large frying pan (skillet), add the onion mixture and fry gently for 2 minutes, stirring all the time. Add the yogurt, cream and 2 tablespoons of the mint and mix well.

5 Add the fried potatoes and stir until coated in the sauce. Cook for a further 5–7 minutes or until heated through and the sauce has thickened, stirring frequently. Season with salt and pepper to taste and sprinkle with the remaining mint and sliced spring onions (scallions). Serve immediately.

Kashmiri Spinach

This is an imaginative way to serve spinach, which adds a little zip to it. It is a very simple dish, and will complement almost any curry.

SERVES 4

500g/1lb spinach (Swiss chard or baby leaf spinach may be substituted)
2 tbsp mustard oil
¼ tsp Garam Masala (see page 4)
1 tsp yellow mustard seeds
2 spring onions (scallions), sliced

1 Remove the tough stalks from the spinach.

2 Heat the mustard oil in a wok or large heavy frying pan (skillet) until it smokes. Add the garam masala and mustard seeds. Cover the pan quickly – you will hear the mustard seeds popping inside.

3 When the popping has ceased, remove the cover, add the spring onions (scallions) and stir in the spinach until wilted.

4 Continue cooking the spinach, uncovered, over a medium heat for 10–15 minutes, until most of the water has evaporated. If using frozen spinach, it will not need as much cooking – cook it until most of the water has evaporated.

5 Remove the spinach and spring onions (scallions) with a perforated spoon in order to drain off any remaining liquid. This dish is more pleasant to eat when it is served as dry as possible. Serve immediately while it is piping hot.

Yellow Split Pea Casserole

If ever there was a winter warmer, this is it – satisfying, and ideal for serving with a lightweight dish such as pilau or biryani.

Serves 4

2 tbsp ghee • 1 tsp black mustard seeds
1 onion, chopped finely • 2 garlic cloves, crushed
1 carrot, grated • 2.5 cm / 1 inch piece of ginger root, grated
1 green chilli, deseeded and chopped finely
1 tbsp tomato purée (paste)
250 g / 8 oz / 1 cup yellow split peas, soaked in
water for 2 hours and drained
425 g / 14 oz can of chopped tomatoes
500 ml / 16 fl oz / 2 cups vegetable stock
250 g / 8 oz / 1½ cups pumpkin, cubed
250 g / 8 oz cauliflower, cut into florets • 2 tbsp oil
1 large aubergine (eggplant), cubed
1 tbsp chopped fresh coriander (cilantro)
1 tsp Garam Masala (see page 4) • salt and pepper

1 Melt the ghee over a medium heat in a large pan. Add the mustard seeds, and when they start to splutter, add the onion, garlic, carrot, and ginger. Cook until soft, about 5 minutes. Add the chilli and stir in the tomato purée (paste). Stir in the split peas. Add the tomatoes and stock, and bring to the boil. Season well. Simmer for 40 minutes, stirring occasionally. Add the pumpkin and cauliflower, and simmer for a further 30 minutes, covered, until the split peas are soft.

2 Meanwhile, heat the oil in a frying pan (skillet) over a high heat. Add the aubergine (eggplant), and stir until sealed on all sides. Remove and drain on paper towels.

3 Stir the aubergine (eggplant) into the split pea mixture with the

coriander (cilantro) and
garam masala.

4 Transfer to a serving dish
and serve immediately.

Channa Dal

This is a dish to consider next time you prepare a dal. Many types of dal (dried pulses and lentils) are used in India – yellow split peas is just one.

SERVES 4

2 tbsp ghee • 1 large onion, chopped finely
1 garlic clove, crushed • 1 tbsp grated ginger root
1 tbsp cumin seeds, ground • 1 dried red chilli
2 tsp coriander seeds, ground
2.5 cm/1 inch piece cinnamon stick
1 tsp salt
½ tsp ground turmeric
250 g/½ lb/2 cups yellow split peas,
soaked in cold water for 1 hour and drained
425 g/14 oz can of plum tomatoes
300 ml/½ pint/1¼ cups water
2 tsp Garam Masala (see page 4)

1 Heat the ghee in a large saucepan, add the onion, garlic and ginger and fry for 3–4 minutes until the onion has softened slightly.

2 Add the cumin, chilli, coriander, cinnamon, salt and turmeric, then stir in the split peas and mix well.

3 Add the tomatoes, breaking them up slightly with the back of a wooden spoon.

4 Add the water and bring to the boil. Reduce the heat to very low and simmer, uncovered, for about 40 minutes, stirring occasionally, until most of the liquid has been absorbed and the split peas are tender. Skim the surface occasionally with a perforated spoon to remove any scum.

5 Gradually stir in the garam masala, tasting after each addition, until it is of the required flavour.

Brindil Bhaji

This is one of the most delicious of the bhaji dishes, and has a wonderful sweet spicy flavour.

SERVES 4

500 g/ 1 lb aubergines (eggplant),
cut into 1 cm/ ½ inch slices
2 tbsp ghee
1 onion, sliced thinly
2 garlic cloves, sliced thinly
2.5 cm/ 1 inch piece of ginger root, grated
½ tsp ground turmeric
1 dried red chilli
½ tsp salt
425 g/ 14 oz can of tomatoes
1 tsp Garam Masala (see page 4)
sprigs of fresh coriander (cilantro), to garnish

1 Cut the aubergine (eggplant) slices into finger-width strips using a sharp knife.

2 Heat the ghee in a saucepan and cook the onion over a medium heat for 7–8 minutes, stirring constantly, until very soft.

3 Add the garlic and aubergine (eggplant), increase the heat and cook for 2 minutes.

4 Stir in the ginger, turmeric, chilli, salt and the tomatoes. Use the back of a wooden spoon to break up the tomatoes. Simmer uncovered for 15–20 minutes until the aubergine (eggplant) is very soft.

5 Stir in the garam masala and simmer for a further 4–5 minutes.

6 Serve garnished with sprigs of fresh coriander (cilantro).

Peshwari Naan

A tandoor oven throws out a ferocious heat; for an authentic effect, leave your grill (broiler) on for a long time before starting.

SERVES 4

50 ml/2 fl oz/¼ cup warm water
pinch of sugar • ½ tsp active dried yeast
500 g/1 lb/4 cups strong white flour • ½ tsp salt
50 ml/2 fl oz/¼ cup natural yogurt
2 crisp, green apples, peeled, cooked and puréed
60 g/2 oz/⅓ cup sultanas (golden raisins)
60 g/2 oz/½ cup flaked (slivered) almonds
1 tbsp coriander (cilantro) leaves • 2 tbsp grated coconut

1 Combine the water and sugar in a bowl and sprinkle over the yeast. Leave for 5–10 minutes, until the yeast has dissolved and the mixture is foamy.

2 Put the flour and salt into a large bowl and make a well in the centre. Pour in the yeast mixture and yogurt to the bowl. Draw the flour into the liquid, until all the flour is absorbed. Mix together, adding enough tepid water to form a soft dough, about 150 ml/¼ pint/⅔ cup. Turn out on to a floured board and knead for 10 minutes until smooth and elastic. Put into an oiled bowl, cover with a cloth and leave for 3 hours in a warm place, or in the fridge overnight. Line the grill (broiler) pan with foil, shiny side up.

3 Divide the dough into 4 pieces and roll each piece out to a 20 cm/8 inch oval on a floured surface. Pull one end out into a teardrop shape, about 5 mm/¼ inch thick. Prick all over with a fork.

4 Brush both sides of the bread with oil. Place under a preheated grill (broiler) at the highest setting. Cook for 3 minutes, turn the bread over and cook for a

further 3 minutes until lightly
browned all over.

5 Spread a teaspoonful of
the apple purée all over
the bread, then sprinkle over
a quarter of the sultanas
(golden raisins), the flaked
(slivered) almonds, the
coriander (cilantro) leaves and
the coconut. Repeat with the
remaining 3 ovals of dough.

Mango Ice Cream

This delicious ice cream makes the perfect ending to a hot and spicy meal.

SERVES 4

150 ml/¼ pint/⅔ cup single (light) cream • 2 egg yolks
½ tsp cornflour (cornstarch) • 1 tsp water
2 × 425 g/14 oz cans of mango slices in syrup, drained
1 tbsp lime or lemon juice
150 ml/¼ pint/⅔ cup double (heavy) cream
sprigs of mint, to decorate

1 Heat the cream in a saucepan until hot (not allowing it to boil). Place the egg yolks in a bowl with the cornflour (cornstarch) and water and mix until smooth. Pour the cream on to the egg yolk mixture, while stirring.

2 Return the mixture to the pan and place over a low heat, stirring constantly until the mixture thickens and coats the back of a wooden spoon (do not hurry this process or the mixture will overcook). Pour into a bowl.

3 Purée the drained mango slices in a blender or food processor until smooth, or chop finely, mash with a fork and push through a sieve. Mix with the custard and stir in the lime juice. Whip the double (heavy) cream until peaks form. Fold into the mango mixture.

4 Transfer the mixture to a loaf tin or shallow freezerproof container. Cover and freeze for 2–3 hours or until half-frozen. Turn the mixture into a bowl and mash well with a fork until smooth. Return to the container, cover and freeze again until firm.

5 Transfer the container of ice cream to the main compartment of the refrigerator for about 30 minutes before serving. Scoop or spoon the ice cream into serving dishes and decorate with sprigs of mint.

Saffron-Spiced Rice Pudding

This rich and comforting pudding is cooked in milk delicately flavoured with saffron and cinnamon.

SERVES 4–5

600 ml / 1 pint / 2½ cups milk
several pinches of saffron strands, finely crushed
60 g / 2 oz / ¼ cup short-grain (pudding) rice
1 cinnamon stick or piece of cassia bark
45 g / 1½ oz / 3 tbsp sugar
30 g / 1 oz / ¼ cup seedless raisins or sultanas (golden raisins)
30 g / 1 oz / ¼ cup ready-soaked dried apricots, chopped
1 egg, beaten
75 ml / 3 fl oz / ⅓ cup single (light) cream
15 g / ½ oz / 1 tbsp butter, diced
15 g / ½ oz / 2 tbsp flaked (slivered) almonds
freshly grated nutmeg, for sprinkling
cream (optional), to serve

1 Place the milk and crushed saffron in a non-stick saucepan and bring to the boil. Stir in the rice and cinnamon stick, reduce the heat and simmer very gently, uncovered, for 25 minutes, stirring frequently until the rice is tender.

2 Remove the pan from the heat and discard the cinnamon stick. Stir in the sugar, raisins and apricots, then beat in the egg, cream and diced butter.

3 Transfer the mixture to a greased ovenproof pie or flan dish, sprinkle with the almonds and freshly grated nutmeg, to taste. Place in a preheated oven, 160°C/325°F/Gas Mark 3, for 25–30 minutes until set and lightly golden. Serve hot with extra cream, if wished.

Sweet Carrot Halva

**This nutritious dessert, made from
grated carrots simmered in milk,
is flavoured with spices, nuts
and raisins.**

SERVES 4

750 g/ 1½ lb carrots, grated
750 ml/ 1¼ pints/ 3 cups milk
1 cinnamon stick or piece of cassia bark (optional)
4 tbsp vegetable ghee or oil
60 g/ 2 oz/ ⅓ cup sugar
30 g/ 1 oz/ ¼ cup unsalted pistachio nuts, chopped
*30–50 g/ 1–2 oz/ ¼–½ cup blanched almonds,
flaked (slivered) or chopped*
60 g/ 2 oz/ ⅓ cup seedless raisins
seeds from 8 cardamom pods, crushed
double (heavy) cream or yogurt, to serve

1 Put the grated carrots, milk and cinnamon or cassia, if using, into a large, heavy-based saucepan and bring to the boil. Reduce the heat to a simmer and cook, uncovered, for 35–40 minutes, or until thickened (with no milk remaining). Stir the mixture frequently during cooking to prevent it sticking. Remove the cinnamon stick.

2 Heat the ghee or oil in a non-stick frying pan (skillet), add the carrot mixture and stir-fry over a medium heat for about 5 minutes or until the carrots take on a glossy sheen.

3 Add the sugar, pistachios, almonds, raisins and crushed cardamom seeds, mix well and continue frying for a further 3–4 minutes, stirring frequently. Serve warm or cold with cream or yogurt.

Index